Indonesia

Sue Townsend and Caroline Young

Heinemann
LIBRARY

www.heinemann.co.uk/library
Visit our website to find out more information about **Heinemann Library** books.

To order:
☎ Phone 44 (0) 1865 888066
▤ Send a fax to 44 (0) 1865 314091
▢ Visit the Heinemann Bookshop at www.heinemann.co.uk/library to browse our catalogue and order online.

First published in Great Britain by Heinemann Library, Halley Court, Jordan Hill, Oxford OX2 8EJ, part of Harcourt Education.

Heinemann is a registered trademark of Harcourt Education Ltd.

Editorial: Nancy Dickmann, Andrew Solway and Jennifer Tubbs
Design: Jo Hinton-Malivoire and Tinstar Design Limited (www.tinstar.co.uk)
Illustrations: Nicholas Beresford-Davies
Picture Research: Catherine Bevan
Production: Séverine Ribierre

Originated by Dot Gradations Ltd
Printed in China
by Wing King Tong

ISBN 0 431 11725 X
07 06 05 04 03
10 9 8 7 6 5 4 3 2 1

British Library Cataloguing in Publication Data
Townsend, Sue & Young, Caroline
Indonesia. – (A World of Recipes)
641.5'123'09598
A full catalogue record for this book is available from the British Library.

Acknowledgements
The publishers would like to thank the following for permission to reproduce photographs: Corbis: p. **5**; Gareth Boden: all other photographs.

Cover photographs reproduced with permission of Gareth Boden.

The publishers would like to thank Diyan Parahitani for her assistance with the preparation of this book.

Every effort has been made to contact copyright holders of any material reproduced in this book. Any omissions will be rectified in subsequent printings if notice is given to the publishers.

Contents

Key

* easy

** medium

*** difficult

Words appearing in the text in bold, **like this**, are explained in the glossary.

Indonesian food

feet HEIGHT metres	
over 13120	over 4000
6560–13120	2000–4000
3277–6557	1000–1999
1640–3277	500–999
656–1637	200–499
under 656	under 200

Indonesia is in south-east Asia. It is made up of more than 17,000 islands, but people only live on 6000 of them. This chain of islands is called an **archipelago**, and it stretches across the ocean between Malaysia to the north-west and Australia to the south-east.

In the past

Throughout the centuries, many different people have visited the islands of Indonesia. Sailors from Malaysia left the mainland in small boats and landed there more than 4000 years ago. Traders from China, India and Arabia settled there, bringing their customs and cooking styles. In 1602, traders from the Netherlands took control of the islands, naming them the Dutch East Indies. They took over all farming, including growing spices such as nutmeg, cloves and peppers – the islands' most important trade. Most of Indonesia became independent in 1949. Today, many people live in Indonesia's busy cities, but in the countryside, people live in a more traditional way.

Rice is the most important crop in Indonesia. The rice grows in flooded paddy fields, but before harvesting the fields are drained.

Around the country

It is hot nearly all year round in Indonesia. The main difference in the weather from place to place is how much rain falls. In many areas, the **monsoon** wind from China brings very heavy rain from December to March. From June to September, a dry wind from Australia blows across the islands, and little rain falls. High mountain ranges, dotted with volcanoes and rainforests, cover many of the islands.

Rice is Indonesia's most important crop. In Java, farmers can grow two or three crops of rice a year. On Java and on other islands further east, farmers grow coconuts, tobacco or palm oil trees on large **plantations**. Fishing is very important for people living on Indonesia's long coastline.

Indonesian meals

Indonesian meals are usually made up of several dishes laid out on the table at the same time. People take a spoonful of rice, then choose some of the other dishes. Food is often hot and spicy, with coriander, pepper and garlic the most important flavours.

Ingredients

pineapple

mango

ginger

beansprouts

coconut milk

lemon grass

chillies

ginger

peanuts

coriander leaves

shrimp paste

Bean sprouts

Bean sprouts grow from mung beans. You can buy them at supermarkets or greengrocers. Always buy bean sprouts that look fresh and crisp.

Candlenuts

Candlenuts look like large, pale hazelnuts. They make people sick if eaten raw, so they are **ground** up and added to sauces. If you cannot find them, use brazil nuts.

Chillies

Indonesian recipes often contain chillies. If you don't like spicy food, add less chilli than suggested, or leave it out. Most supermarkets sell chillies fresh, **chopped** and packed in jars, or dried. Use small chillies, labelled chilli peppers, not bird's eye chillies. Throw away the seeds, and wash your hands thoroughly after touching them – chilli juice can make your eyes and skin very sore.

Coriander

The leaves, root and seeds of the coriander herb are used to flavour many Indonesian dishes. Each part of the coriander plant has a slightly different flavour.

Coconut milk

Coconut milk is made from coconut flesh, not the liquid inside a fresh coconut. You can buy coconut milk in cans, or as a powder.

Fresh ginger

Fresh ginger is a root, which is **peeled** and **grated**. It adds a warm, slightly lemony flavour to dishes. Most supermarkets sell it. You cannot use dried, ground ginger for the recipes in this book.

Lemon grass

Lemon grass has a delicate, lemony flavour. Indonesian cooks use it to flavour many dishes.

Palm sugar

This sugar is made from the juice of the coconut palm flower. It is dark brown and very hard. Use dark brown sugar instead if you cannot find palm sugar.

Peanuts

Peanuts are also called groundnuts. Indonesian cooks use them to flavour foods and thicken sauces. Use peanuts that have not been **roasted**, unless the recipe says so.

Shrimp paste

This strongly flavoured paste is made from crushed shrimps, and is very salty. If you cannot find it, use anchovy essence instead.

Before you start

Kitchen rules

There are a few basic rules you should always follow when you are cooking:

- Ask an adult if you can use the kitchen.
- Some cooking processes, especially those involving hot water or oil, can be dangerous. When you see this sign, take extra care or ask an adult to help.
- Wash your hands before you start.
- Wear an apron to protect your clothes.
- Be very careful when you use sharp knives.
- Never leave pan handles sticking out, in case you knock them.
- Use oven gloves to lift things in and out of the oven.
- Wash fruits and vegetables before you use them.
- Always wash chopping boards very well after use, especially after chopping raw meat, fish or poultry.
- Use a separate chopping board for onions and garlic, if possible.

How long will it take?

Some of the recipes in this book are quick and easy, and some are more difficult and take longer. The strip across the right-hand side of each recipe page tells you how long it takes to prepare a dish from start to finish. It also shows how difficult it is to make – each recipe is * (easy), ** (medium) or *** (difficult).

Quantities and measurements

You can see how many people each recipe will serve at the top of each right-hand page. You can multiply or divide the quantities if you want to cook for more or fewer people.

Ingredients for recipes can be measured in two different ways. Metric measurements use grams and millilitres. Imperial measurements use ounces and fluid ounces. This book uses metric measurements. If you want to convert these into imperial measurements, see the chart on page 44.

In the recipes, you will see the following abbreviations:

tbsp = tablespoon   g = grams
tsp = teaspoon   ml = millilitres

Utensils

To cook the recipes in this book, you will need these utensils (as well as essentials, such as spoons, plates and bowls):

- plastic or glass chopping board (easier to clean than wooden ones)
- food processor or blender
- large frying pan
- 20 cm non-stick frying pan
- 18 cm non-stick frying pan (heavy-based if possible)
- lemon squeezer
- measuring jug
- wok or large saucepan with lid
- small saucepan with lid
- sieve
- set of scales
- grater
- sharp knife
- palette knife
- baking sheets
- steamer or metal colander
- wooden **skewers**.

 Whenever you use kitchen knives, be very careful.

Peanut fritters

In Indonesia, street traders sell these fritters as take-away food. They are called *rempeyk kacang* (pronounced *rum-PAY-ek-kah-chang*). You can serve them on their own as a snack, or with other dishes as part of a meal.

What you need

1 clove garlic
50 g **roasted** salted peanuts
50 g rice flour
½ tsp **ground** coriander
½ tsp ground cumin
½ tsp ground turmeric
½ tsp baking powder
6 tbsp coconut milk
1 tbsp groundnut or vegetable oil

What you do

1 **Peel** and finely **chop** or crush the garlic.

2 Put the peanuts into a blender, and **blend** briefly until roughly chopped.

3 Put the garlic, peanuts, rice flour, coriander, cumin, turmeric and baking powder into a bowl.

4 Stir the coconut milk and 9 tbsp water together in a jug. Add the liquid to the peanut mixture.

⚠ 5 Heat the oil in a large frying pan over a medium heat. Put 1 tbsp of peanut mixture into the pan.

6 Add three or four more fritters to the pan, leaving a space between then. **Fry** for 2 minutes, until the mixture looks set.

7 Use a palette knife or a fish slice to turn the fritters over, and cook for a further 2 minutes, until they are golden brown.

8 Lift the cooked fritters on to kitchen paper to **drain** while you cook the rest of the mixture. Serve the fritters hot or cold.

GROUNDNUT OIL

Many Indonesian dishes are cooked in groundnut oil, which is made from peanuts. If you cannot find groundnut oil, use vegetable oil instead.

11

Peanut sauce

Indonesian people often serve spicy sauces, called sambals, with their meals. Try serving this peanut sauce with Chicken satay (see page 22) or with Vegetable gado-gado (page 14). You can keep it in a clean jar in the fridge for up to three days.

What you need

1 clove garlic
1 small onion
½ red chilli (if you like it)
400 g raw peanuts (not **roasted**) in their shells or 200 g shelled raw peanuts
4 tbsp vegetable or groundnut oil
1 tsp shrimp paste or anchovy essence
1 tsp palm sugar or brown sugar
1 tbsp dark soy sauce

What you do

1 **Peel** the garlic and onion, and **chop** them finely.

2 Cut the piece of chilli in half and throw away the seeds. Chop the chilli finely. Wash your hands well after handling raw chilli.

3 Take the peanuts out of their shells, if necessary.

(!) 4 Heat the oil in a wok over a medium heat. Add the peanuts and cook for 3–4 minutes, stirring all the time. Turn the heat off.

5 Using a slotted spoon, lift the peanuts into a bowl, leaving the oil in the wok.

(!) **6** Heat the wok again over a medium heat, and **fry** the garlic, onion and chilli for 1 minute. Turn the heat off, and spoon them into the bowl with the peanuts.

7 Put the peanuts and onion mixture into a blender, and **blend** until smooth. Empty the mixture into a saucepan.

8 Stir the shrimp paste, sugar, soy sauce and 225 ml water into the peanut mixture. Cook over a low heat, stirring all the time, until it is **simmering**. Simmer for 3 minutes, then serve hot or cold.

Vegetable gado-gado

This dish is a favourite in Indonesian restaurants around the world. In Indonesia, street traders sell it wrapped in banana leaves as a snack. Serve it with Peanut sauce (see page 12).

What you need

150 g medium-sized
 potatoes
pinch of salt
4 eggs
half a cucumber
100 g spinach
100 g white cabbage
100 g bean sprouts
100 g beancurd
2 tbsp groundnut or
 vegetable oil
50 g packet ready-
 cooked prawn crackers

What you do

(!) **1** **Peel** the potatoes. Put them in a pan with a pinch of salt. Cover them with **boiling** water, and cook for 20 minutes. When cooked, **drain** them and cover them with cold water.

2 Put the eggs into a pan, cover with boiling water, and **simmer** them for 8 minutes. Lift them into a bowl of cold water.

3 Cut the cucumber into 1 cm slices, then cut each into four. Put them into a sieve, sprinkle with salt and leave the sieve over a bowl.

4 Wash the spinach and pat it dry. Finely **shred** the spinach and white cabbage.

(!) **5** Pour boiling water into a large saucepan. Add the cabbage and bring back to the boil. Add the spinach and bean sprouts and drain immediately.

6 Cover the vegetables with cold water, then drain again.

(!) 7 Cut the beancurd into 1 cm cubes. Heat the oil in a frying pan or wok, and **fry** the beancurd for 2–3 minutes. Carefully lift the beancurd on to kitchen paper.

8 Peel the shells off the eggs. Cut them into quarters.

9 Rinse the cucumber wedges and leave them to drain.

10 Cut the potatoes into 2 cm cubes.

11 Arrange all the ingredients on a plate. Serve with prawn crackers and Peanut sauce (see page 12).

Crab and baby sweetcorn soup

In Indonesia, people serve soup with all their other dishes. If the other food on the table is spicy, the soup is made less hot to balance the flavours.

What you need

6 spring onions
200 g baby sweetcorn
3 cm piece fresh ginger
100 g beancurd
1 tbsp groundnut or
   vegetable oil
pinch of chilli powder
   (if you like it)
1 chicken stock cube
1 tbsp caster sugar
1 tbsp light soy sauce
170 g can white crab
   meat
3 tbsp fresh coriander

What you do

1 Trim both ends from the spring onions. Finely **slice** the white part of the onion, then the green part, keeping them separate.

2 Cut the baby sweetcorn into 1 cm pieces. **Peel** the ginger and cut it into 3 slices.

3 Cut the beancurd into 1½ cm cubes.

(!) 4 Heat the oil in a saucepan over a medium heat. **Fry** the white part of the spring onions for 2 minutes. Add the sweetcorn, ginger, beancurd and chilli powder, and cook for 2 minutes, stirring all the time.

(!) 5 Lift the beancurd out on to kitchen paper. Crumble the stock cube and add it to the pan, with the sugar, soy sauce and 600 ml hot water. **Cover** the pan and **simmer** for 15 minutes.

6 Using a slotted spoon, lift out the pieces of ginger and throw them away.

7 Add the crab meat, beancurd and green spring onion tops. Cook for 3 minutes.

8 **Chop** the coriander and stir into the soup. Serve straightaway.

Prawn and rice noodle soup

This filling soup is made with meat, vegetables and thin noodles made from rice flour, called *miehun* (pronounced *mee-hoon*) in Indonesia.

What you need

1 chicken breast
5 spring onions
1 clove garlic
5 cm piece fresh ginger
1 chicken stock cube
1 tbsp groundnut or vegetable oil
1 tsp **ground** coriander
¼ tsp ground turmeric
175 g rice noodles
300 ml coconut milk
75 g bean sprouts
150 g peeled prawns

What you do

(!) **1** Put the chicken into a pan and cover it with water. **Cover** the pan, bring the water to the **boil**, and **simmer** for 20 minutes.

2 Meanwhile, trim both ends off the spring onions. Finely **slice** the white and green parts, keeping them separate.

3 **Peel** the garlic and crush, or finely **chop**, it.

4 Peel and finely **grate** the ginger.

5 Using a slotted spoon, lift the chicken breast on to a board to cool. Keep the cooking liquid.

6 Cut the cooked chicken into thin slices.

7 Crumble the stock cube into a measuring jug. Add the chicken liquid and water to make 500 ml.

(!) **8** Heat the oil in a wok or saucepan. **Stir-fry** the white part of the spring onions for 1 minute. Add the garlic, ginger, coriander and turmeric, and stir-fry for 30 seconds.

9 Add the chicken, and stir-fry for 1 minute. Pour in the stock and bring the soup to the boil. Cover and simmer for 20 minutes.

⓵ 10 Put the noodles into a pan of boiling water for 5 minutes, then **drain** them.

11 Stir in the noodles and coconut milk. Add the bean sprouts, prawns and green spring onion tops. Simmer for 3 minutes and serve.

Nasi goreng

In Indonesia, this dish of fried rice, chicken, beef and prawns, is often served **garnished** with onion rings and strips of omelette as a delicious meal.

What you need

300 g basmati rice
 or fragrant Thai rice
1 chicken breast
200 g beef fillet
1–2 fresh red chillies
    (if you like them)
2 cloves garlic
1 onion
2 tbsp groundnut or
    vegetable oil
100 g peeled prawns
2 tbsp dark soy sauce
1 tsp shrimp paste or
    anchovy essence

To garnish:
For omelette strips:
2 eggs
salt and pepper
1 tbsp groundnut or
    vegetable oil

For Crispy onion rings:
1 onion
2 tbsp groundnut or
    vegetable oil

What you do

(!) 1 Put the rice in a pan with 600 ml **boiling** water. Bring back to the boil and **simmer** for 20 minutes.

2 **Drain** the rice in a sieve. Put it over a bowl and run cold water over the rice.

(!) 3 Put the chicken breast into a small pan. **Cover** with water and bring it to the boil. Cover and simmer for 20 minutes.

4 Make the omelette strips (see 6–9 on page 39) and Crispy onion rings (see page 25).

5 Lift the chicken on to a board to cool, then cut it into thin strips.

6 Cut the beef fillet into thin slices.

7 Cut the chillies in half and throw away the seeds. **Chop** the chilli finely, then wash your hands.

8 **Peel** and chop, or crush, the garlic. Peel and **slice** the onion into rings.

9 Put the onion, chilli and garlic into a blender, and **blend** until smooth.

(!) 10 Heat the oil in a wok and **fry** the blended mixture for 1 minute. Add the beef and **stir-fry** for 2 minutes. Add the prawns and chicken, and stir-fry for 2 minutes.

11 Add the rice, soy sauce and shrimp paste. Cook for 5 minutes.

12 Spoon the mixture on to a serving plate. Serve, garnished with omelette strips and onion rings.

Chicken satay

Indonesian cooks make satay with a spice called *bumbu lengkap*. Street traders sell satay as a snack, and people buy it to eat as part of a main meal. Serve it with Peanut sauce (see page 12).

What you need

1 onion
2 cloves garlic
2 candlenuts or
    brazil nuts
1 stem lemon grass
½ tsp chilli powder
    (if you like it)
1 tsp **ground** coriander
1 tsp ground cumin
pinch of ground cloves
1 tsp ground cinnamon
½ tsp ground nutmeg
½ tsp ground turmeric
2 tbsp groundnut oil
    or vegetable oil
1 tsp shrimp paste or
    anchovy essence
3 skinless, boneless
    chicken breasts

To garnish:
half a cucumber

What you do

1 **Peel** and **chop** the onion and garlic. Crush or chop the nuts.

2 Cut the root off the lemon grass, peel off the outside layer and chop the middle section.

3 Put the chilli powder, coriander, cumin, cloves, cinnamon, nutmeg and turmeric into a bowl.

(!) 4 Heat the oil in a wok or saucepan over a medium heat. **Fry** the onion for 3 minutes. Add the garlic and cook for 1 minute.

5 Add the lemon grass and spices, and cook for 30 seconds. Cook slightly and spoon the mixture into a blender.

6 Add the shrimp paste and 2 tbsp water, and **blend** to a smooth paste.

22

7 On a board, cut the chicken into 2 cm pieces. Put them into a bowl.

8 Stir the blended mixture into the chicken. **Cover** and **chill** for 2 hours.

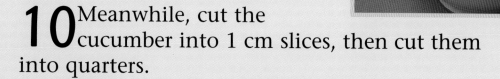

9 Soak 8 wooden skewers in cold water for 30 minutes.

10 Meanwhile, cut the cucumber into 1 cm slices, then cut them into quarters.

⊘ 11 Push the chicken pieces on to the skewers.

⊘ 12 **Preheat** a grill to medium hot. **Grill** the satay for 5–7 minutes, turning them over halfway through. Serve with Peanut sauce (see page 12), garnished with cucumber quarters.

Aromatic chicken

In Indonesia, this dish is often prepared for a feast or special occasion. It tastes even better if you **chill** it overnight – but let it cool before you put it into the fridge. **Reheat** it in a saucepan until it is piping hot, before serving with basmati or fragrant Thai rice.

What you need

1 tbsp **ground** coriander
1 tsp ground cumin
½ tsp ground cloves
½ tsp ground nutmeg
½ tsp ground turmeric
1 onion
3 cm piece fresh ginger
1 chicken stock cube
225 ml water
8 boneless chicken thighs
   or 4 chicken breasts cut
   in half
1 tbsp groundnut oil or
   vegetable oil

To garnish:
Crispy onion rings:
1 onion
2 tbsp groundnut or
   vegetable oil

What you do

1 **Dry-fry** the spices in a frying pan for 30 seconds. Tip the spices into a blender.

2 **Peel** and roughly **chop** the onion and the ginger. Add them to the blender, and **blend** until smooth.

3 Crumble the stock cube into the blender. Add half the water and blend again.

4 Pour the spice mixture over the chicken in a bowl. **Cover** the bowl with cling film and chill for 2 hours.

5 Heat the oil in a saucepan over a medium heat. Using **tongs**, lift the chicken pieces into the pan, and **fry** for 2–3 minutes on each side. Add the rest of the water and spice mixture in the bowl, and stir well.

6 Cook over a medium heat until **boiling**. Cover and **simmer** for 50 minutes.

7 Serve hot with rice and Crispy onion rings (see box).

CRISPY ONION RINGS

Crispy onion rings are used to garnish many Indonesian dishes. Indonesians use shallot-like onions, but you can use ordinary onions. You need:

1 onion
2 tbsp groundnut or vegetable oil

1 Peel and **slice** the onion thinly.

2 Heat 2 tbsp oil in a frying pan. Fry the onion rings over a medium heat for 5 minutes, until crispy. Lift on to kitchen paper, then serve.

Spiced beef and coconut stew

This recipe uses beef, but traditionally it is made with buffalo meat. If you cannot buy the root galangal, use fresh ginger and lemon juice for a similar flavour.

What you need

1 onion
2 cloves garlic
3 cm piece fresh galangal
    or 3 cm piece fresh ginger
    and 2 tbsp lemon juice
3 cm piece fresh ginger
1–2 red chillies (optional)
1 stem lemon grass
½ tsp ground turmeric
½ tsp ground coriander
½ tsp ground cumin
500 g braising steak
1 lime leaf (optional)
1 tsp ready-prepared
    tamarind paste
    or dash lemon juice
400 ml can coconut milk
2 tbsp groundnut or
    vegetable oil
6 new potatoes

*To **garnish**:*
Crispy onion rings:
1 onion
2 tbsp groundnut or
    vegetable oil

What you do

1 **Peel** and roughly **chop** the onion and garlic. Peel and **slice** the galangal and ginger.

2 Cut the chillies in half and throw away the seeds. Chop the chilli finely, washing your hands thoroughly afterwards.

3 Cut the root off the lemon grass. Peel off the tough outer layer. Chop the middle section finely.

4 Put the onion, garlic, galangal, ginger, lemon grass, chilli, turmeric, coriander and cumin into a blender and **blend** until smooth.

5 Trim any fat from the beef, and cut it into 3 cm cubes. Mix the beef and spice paste together in a bowl.

6 Tear the lime leaf (if using) into 4 pieces. Add them to the beef, cover the bowl with cling film and **chill** for 2 hours.

7 Put the tamarind paste, or a dash of lemon or lime juice, into a jug. Stir in the coconut milk and 100 ml water.

8 Heat the oil in a wok, and **fry** the meat over a high heat for 3 minutes.

9 Stir in the coconut milk mixture and bring to the **boil**. **Cover** and **simmer** for 1½ hours.

10 Wash the potatoes and add them to the pan. Cook for 20 minutes.

11 Serve with basmati or fragrant Thai rice, garnished with Crispy onion rings (see page 25).

Steamed cabbage with coconut

In Indonesia, cooks **steam** food in a bamboo steamer resting over a wok full of **boiling** water. This is very healthy, because it uses no fat. If you do not have a steamer, rest a metal colander over a pan of boiling water.

What you need

white flesh of half
   a coconut
400 g white cabbage
 or 1 large head
   Chinese leaf
½ red chilli (if you like it)
2 cloves garlic
1 lime
1 tsp palm sugar or
   brown sugar
2 tsp shrimp paste or
   anchovy essence

What you do

(!) 1 Wrap the coconut in a tea towel and put it on the floor outside. Tap the coconut with a hammer until it cracks, then pull it apart. Let the see-through fluid **drain** away, and cut off the hard brown shell.

2 Using a grater, **grate** half the flesh from inside the coconut.

3 If using white cabbage, cut it into quarters. Cut out the hard stem and throw it away. **Shred** the cabbage. If using Chinese leaf, cut off the base and shred the leaves.

4 Cut the chilli in half and throw away the seeds. **Chop** the chilli finely, washing your hands thoroughly afterwards.

5 **Peel** and crush, or chop, the garlic. Using a lemon squeezer, squeeze the juice from the lime.

6 Bring a large pan of water to the boil.

7 **Toss** the cabbage or Chinese leaf and chilli together in a bowl. Put them into a steamer. **Cover** the steamer and place it carefully over the pan of boiling water. Steam for 3 minutes for slightly crunchy vegetables, or longer, if you prefer.

8 Mix the coconut, garlic, lime juice, sugar and shrimp paste together. Put the cabbage into a serving bowl and spoon over the coconut mixture. Toss well and serve.

Carrot and mooli salad

In Indonesia, people often serve salads of **grated** vegetables at the same time as other dishes. Their cool, fresh flavours go well with spicier foods. Many supermarkets sell mooli, which is also called white radish. It has a slightly peppery taste.

What you need

5 medium carrots
250 g mooli

*For the **dressing**:*
3 tbsp white wine
  vinegar
1 tbsp caster sugar
½ tsp salt
½ red chilli
  (if you like it)
½ green chilli
  (if you like it)

What you do

1 **Peel** the carrots and the mooli. Cut off both ends. **Chop** the vegetables into pieces about 4 cm long.

2 Cut a thin slice off the side of each piece, so that they lie flat on a chopping board.

3 Cut each piece lengthways into thin slices, then cut the slices the other way, to make matchstick-shaped pieces. Put the pieces into a bowl.

4 Cut the red and green chillies in half, and throw away the seeds. Chop the chillies finely, washing your hands well afterwards.

5 Stir the vinegar, 3 tbsp water, sugar and salt together until the sugar has **dissolved**. Add the chillies.

6 Pour the dressing over the carrot and mooli. **Toss** well, and spoon on to a plate before serving.

ANOTHER VERSION

If you cannot find mooli, you could replace it with the following amounts of bean sprouts or apples:

175 g bean sprouts or 4 large eating apples

1 Rinse the bean sprouts with cold water and pat them dry or peel and coarsely grate the apples.

2 Add to the other ingredients and toss in the dressing. Serve straight away.

Spicy scrambled egg

This simple dish is popular all over Indonesia. People serve it as a snack, or as part of a main meal with other dishes. They add different vegetables, depending on what grows on their island. Either use the vegetables suggested here, or choose your own.

What you need

4 spring onions
3 cm piece fresh
  ginger
2 cloves garlic
1 carrot
50 g green beans
2 eggs
2 tbsp groundnut
  or vegetable oil
170 g can white
  crab meat
1 tbsp soy sauce
pinch of chilli powder
  (if you like it)

What you do

1 Trim both ends from the spring onions. Finely **slice** the white and the green parts, keeping them separate.

2 **Peel** and grate the ginger.

3 Peel and crush, or finely **chop**, the garlic.

4 Peel the carrot and cut off both ends. Cut it into pieces 4 cm long.

5 Cut a thin slice off each piece of carrot so that they lie flat on a chopping board.

6 Cut each piece lengthways into thin slices, then cut the slices the other way, to make thin, matchstick-shaped pieces. Put them into a bowl.

7 Trim the ends off the beans and cut them in half.

8 Crack the eggs into a bowl, and **beat** them lightly with a fork.

! **9** Heat the oil in a wok over a medium heat. **Stir-fry** the white part of the spring onion for 1 minute. Add the ginger, garlic, carrot and beans, and stir-fry for 3 minutes.

10 Add the crab meat, soy sauce and green spring onion tops. Stir-fry for 1 minute.

11 Add the chilli powder and eggs. Stir-fry until the eggs have set. Serve hot.

Sumatran-style lamb chops

Curry is very popular in Indonesia, where it is called *kare* (pronounced *car-RAY*). Cooks often make a large amount of curry at the beginning of the week, and serve it every day with different dishes. Curry recipes from the island of Sumatra are usually medium hot, and are cooked with coconut milk.

What you need

1 small onion
2 cloves garlic
2 cm piece fresh ginger
½ stem lemon grass
½ red chilli (if you like it)
4 candlenuts or brazil nuts
½ tsp **ground** turmeric
salt and pepper
2 tbsp groundnut or
    vegetable oil
4 lean lamb chump chops
2 tbsp lemon juice
1 tsp palm sugar or brown
    sugar
1 tsp ground coriander
225 ml coconut milk

What you do

1 **Peel** and finely **chop** the onion and garlic.

2 Peel and **grate** the ginger over a plate.

3 Cut the root off the lemon grass and peel off the tough outer layer. Chop the middle section finely.

4 Cut the chilli in half and throw away the seeds. Chop the chilli finely, washing your hands well afterwards.

5 Put the onion, garlic, ginger, lemon grass, chilli, nuts and turmeric into a blender. Add salt and pepper, and **blend** until smooth.

6 Heat the oil in a wok, and **fry** the spice mixture over a medium heat for 3 minutes. Add the chops and fry for 2 minutes on each side, until they are brown.

7 Add the lemon juice, sugar, coriander and 225 ml water. Stir well, **cover** and **simmer** for 25 minutes.

8 Stir in the coconut milk, and simmer for 5 more minutes. Serve hot with Festive rice cones (see pages 38–39) or rice noodles.

Beancurd omelettes

Indonesian cooks use chicken and duck eggs to make omelettes. Omelettes can be served as a snack, or rolled up and sliced as a garnish for other dishes (see page 39). This popular omelette recipe adds onion, chilli and beancurd to the eggs.

What you need

1 onion
½ red chilli (if you like it)
50 g beancurd
4 eggs
salt and pepper
2 tbsp groundnut
    or vegetable oil

To garnish:
sprigs of coriander

What you do

1 Peel the onion. Cut off the tip. Holding the root end, cut it into thin **slices**.

2 Cut the chilli in half and throw away the seeds. **Chop** the chilli finely, washing your hands well afterwards.

3 Cut the beancurd into 1 cm cubes.

4 Crack the eggs into a bowl. Add 2 tbsp water and some salt and pepper, and **beat** lightly with a fork.

5 Stir in the onion, chilli and beancurd.

(!) **6** Heat 1 tbsp of the oil in a 20 cm non-stick frying pan over a medium heat for 1 minute. Stir the egg mixture and spoon half of it into the pan.

7 Cook the mixture for 2–3 minutes, until the underside of the omelette is brown when lifted with a fish slice.

8 Using a fish slice, turn the omelette over and cook the other side.

9 Put on to a plate and repeat steps 5–8 to cook the second omelette. Serve garnished with coriander.

FAST FOOD

On the Indonesian island of Madura, local people hold a series of races for bulls every year. Before the racing season starts in August, the bulls are fed beer, eggs and chillies. This diet is said to make them run faster.

Festive rice cone

This dish is often served at Indonesian festivals. The rice is made into a cone shape by being pressed into a conical sieve and then turned upside down on the plate. If you don't have a conical sieve, serve the rice on a plate in a mound-shape.

What you need

1 clove garlic
1 onion
2 tbsp groundnut
   or vegetable oil
½ tsp ground
   turmeric
200 g basmati or
   fragrant Thai rice
225 ml coconut milk
1 stem lemon grass

To garnish:
For omelette strips:
2 eggs
salt and pepper
1 tbsp groundnut
   or vegetable oil
half a cucumber

For Crispy onion rings:
1 onion
2 tbsp groundnut
   or vegetable oil

What you do

1 **Peel** and **chop**, or crush, the garlic.

(!) 2 Peel and **slice** the onion. Heat the oil in a medium saucepan and **fry** over a medium heat for 2 minutes. Add the garlic and fry for 1 minute.

3 Add the turmeric and rice, and cook for 3 minutes, stirring all the time.

(!) 4 Stir in the coconut milk and 300 ml hot water, and bring to the **boil**.

5 Hit the lemon grass with a rolling pin, or bend it a few times to release its flavour. Add it to the rice and **simmer** for 15 minutes, until the liquid has been soaked up. (Add water if the rice sticks.)

6 Crack the eggs into a bowl, and add salt and pepper.

(!) 7 Heat the oil in a frying pan. Pour in half the egg mixture and cook for 2–3 minutes, until the underside of the omelette is brown.

8 Lift the omelette onto a board to cool. Make a second omelette.

9 Roll the omelettes up and cut them into 2 cm slices.

10 Cut the cucumber into thick slices, then cut each slice into quarters.

11 Lift out the lemon grass. Put a conical sieve into a jug or bowl and spoon the rice into the sieve, pressing down well.

12 Tip the rice on to a plate and garnish with omelette strips, Crispy onion rings (see page 25) and cucumber.

Coconut pancakes

Indonesian meals usually finish with fresh fruit, such as bananas or paw paws (papayas). People would only serve desserts like this recipe on special occasions. Indonesian desserts can be very sweet – traditionally, this recipe has double the amount of sugar suggested here.

What you need

For the filling:
5 tbsp dark brown sugar
100 g **desiccated** coconut

For the pancakes:
100 g plain flour
1 egg
300 ml milk
3 tbsp groundnut oil or
  vegetable oil

To garnish:
small piece of fresh
  coconut

What you do

(!) 1 Put the sugar and 175 ml water into a non-stick saucepan. Heat over a low heat until the sugar has dissolved.

2 Add the coconut and cook for 3 minutes, until the coconut has soaked up the liquid. Turn the heat off leave to cool. Turn the oven on to its lowest setting.

3 Put the flour, egg and milk into a blender, and **blend** into a smooth batter.

(!)**4** Heat 1 tbsp of oil in a 20 cm non-stick frying pan over a medium heat. Add 2 tbsp pancake batter, tilting the pan so that it covers the base.

5 Cook for 2 minutes, or until the surface of the batter has set.

6 Using a fish slice, turn the pancake over and cook for 2 minutes.

7 Slide the pancake on to a heatproof plate. **Cover** it with foil and keep it in the oven. Repeat steps 4–6 to make 8 pancakes.

8 Put a spoonful of coconut filling into the middle of each pancake. Roll the pancakes up.

9 Using a vegetable peeler, shave off some **slices** of fresh coconut and scatter them over the pancakes. Serve straight away.

Fruit salad

Many different types of fruit grow on the islands of Indonesia. This dish is a simple fruit salad that might traditionally be served after a meal. It includes a pomelo, but if you cannot find one, try using a grapefruit for a similar flavour.

What you need

1 pineapple
1 mango
1 pomelo
2 bananas

What you do

1 Cut off the top and base off the pineapple. Stand the pineapple on a **chopping** board on one end.

2 Starting from the top, carefully cut large strips of the skin away from the pineapple flesh. Throw away the skin.

3 Cut the pineapple in half and then cut each half again lengthways. Cut off the tough core in the middle of each piece and throw it away. Cut the pineapple flesh into bite-sized pieces.

4 Cut the mango lengthways into three equal pieces. The middle piece will contain the flat stone. **Slice** the fruit flesh into long strips and cut off the skin. Trim any fruit from around the stone.

5 **Peel** the thick skin off the pomelo. Cut the fruit into slices.

6 Peel and cut the bananas into slices.

7 Arrange the fruit on a large plate and serve.

COCONUTS

Coconut is an important ingredient in Indonesian cooking, but coconuts can be used in many other ways. Coconut flesh can be dried and crushed to produce coconut oil. A fibre called coir, made from the husk of the coconut, is used to make carpets, matting and thatching for roofs. The shell of a coconut makes excellent charcoal, too.

Further information

Here are some places to find out more about Indonesia and Indonesian cooking.

Books

Indonesian Food and Cookery, Sri Owen (Piatkus, 1988)
Next Stop: Indonesia, Fred Martin (Heinemann, 1999)
Worldfocus: Indonesia, Susi Arnott (Heinemann, 1996)

Websites

www.asiarecipe.com/indonesia.html
www.cuisinenet.com/glossary/indon.html
www.indochef.com
www.indokitchen.com

Conversion chart

Ingredients for recipes can be measured in two different ways. Metric measurements use grams and millilitres. Imperial measurements use ounces and fluid ounces. This book uses metric measurements. The chart here shows you how to convert measurements from metric to imperial.

SOLIDS		LIQUIDS	
METRIC	IMPERIAL	METRIC	IMPERIAL
10 g	¼ oz	30 ml	1 fl oz
15 g	½ oz	50 ml	2 fl oz
25 g	1 oz	75 ml	2½ fl oz
50 g	1¾ oz	100 ml	3½ fl oz
75 g	2¾ oz	125 ml	4 fl oz
100 g	3½ oz	150 ml	5 fl oz
150 g	5 oz	300 ml	10 fl oz
250 g	9 oz	600 ml	20 fl oz
450 g	16 oz		

Healthy eating

This diagram shows which foods you should eat to stay healthy. Most of your food should come from the bottom of the food pyramid. Eat some of the foods from the middle every day. Only eat a little of the foods from the top.

Healthy eating, Indonesian-style

Indonesian cookery uses a lot of foods that belong in the bottom half of this pyramid. Many dishes blend lightly cooked vegetables with lean meat, such as chicken and fish. Food is often **stir-fried** in a small amount of oil, or cooked in a spicy sauce. Rice is a vital part of most Indonesian meals, because it grows so plentifully. It is served with most savoury dishes, or sweetened with lots of sugar as a dessert.

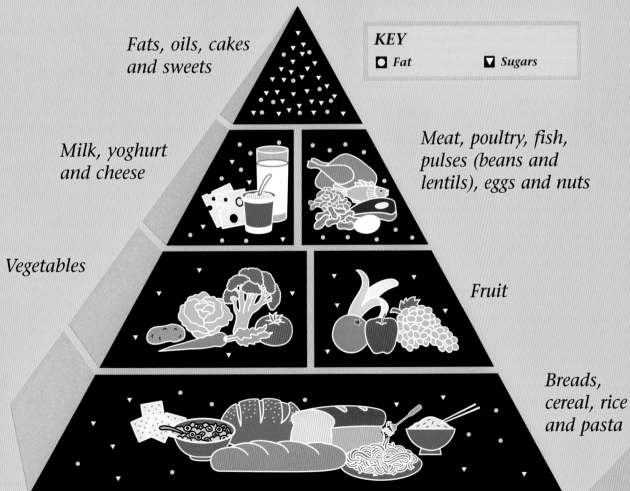

Fats, oils, cakes and sweets

KEY
◻ Fat   ▽ Sugars

Milk, yoghurt and cheese

Meat, poultry, fish, pulses (beans and lentils), eggs and nuts

Vegetables

Fruit

Breads, cereal, rice and pasta

Glossary

archipelago line, or chain, of islands

beat mix ingredients strongly, using a fork or whisk

blend mix ingredients together in an electric blender or food processor

boil cook a liquid on the hob. Boiling liquid bubbles and steams strongly.

chill put a dish in the fridge for a while before serving

chop cut into small pieces using a sharp knife

cover put a lid on a pan, or put foil or cling film over a dish

desiccated in this book, dried, flaked coconut flesh

dissolve mix something, such as sugar, until it disappears into a liquid

drain remove liquid, usually by pouring something into a colander or sieve

dressing sauce for a salad

dry-fry cook over a high heat without any oil

fry cook something in oil in a pan

garnish decorate food, for example, with fresh herbs

grate break something, such as cheese, into small pieces using a grater

grill cook under a grill

ground made into a fine powder

monsoon wind that blows across an area, often bringing heavy rainfall

peel remove the skin of a fruit or vegetable

plantations very large farm which usually only grows one crop

preheat turn on the oven in advance, so that it is hot when you are ready to use it

reheat heat food thoroughly again

roast cook in a hot oven

shred cut or tear something, such as lettuce, into small pieces

simmer cook liquid on the hob. Simmering liquid bubbles and steams gently.

skewer long wooden stick for holding food

slice cut into thin, flat pieces

steam cook in hot steam from boiling water

stir-fry cook foods in a little oil over a high heat, stirring all of the time

tongs u-shaped kitchen utensil used for turning over hot food

toss mix ingredients, for example, in a salad, quite roughly

Index

Titles in the A World of Recipes series include:

Hardback   0431 117268

Hardback   0431 11725X

Hardback   0431 117284

Hardback   0431 117276

Hardback   0431 117306

Hardback   0431 117292

Find out about the other titles in this series on our website www.heinemann.co.uk/library